Animal Activities

KEEPING SAFE

JANE BURTON

**For a free color catalog describing Gareth Stevens' list
of high-quality children's books call 1 (800) 433-0942**

Editors' Note: The use of a capital letter for an animal's name means that it is a species of animal (for example, African Mouthbreeder). The use of a lowercase, or small, letter means that it is a member of a larger group of animals.

Library of Congress Cataloging-in-Publication Data
Burton, Jane.
        Keeping safe / by Jane Burton; photography by Jane Burton and Kim Taylor. --
North American ed.
        p. cm. -- (Animal activities)
        Includes index.
        Summary: Photographs and text depict how animals use teeth, claws, spikes,
horns, camouflage, poison, and other ways to protect themselves from their enemies.
        ISBN 0-8368-0186-5
        1. Animal defenses--Juvenile literature. [1. Animal defenses. 2. Animal weapons.]
I. Taylor, Kim, ill. II. Title. III. Series: Burton, Jane. Animal activities.
QL759.B872   1989
591.57--dc20   89-11416

This North American edition first published in 1989 by

Gareth Stevens Children's Books
7317 W. Green Tree Road
Milwaukee, Wisconsin 53223, USA

Format copyright © 1989 by Gareth Stevens, Inc. Supplementary text copyright
© 1989 by Gareth Stevens, Inc. Original text copyright © 1989 by Jane Burton.
Photographs copyright © 1989 by Jane Burton and Kim Taylor. First published
in Great Britain in 1989 by Belitha Press Ltd.

Editors, U.S.: Patricia Lantier and Valerie Weber

Printed in the United States of America

1 2 3 4 5 6 7 8 9 95 94 93 92 91 90 89

Animal Activities
KEEPING SAFE
JANE BURTON

Gareth Stevens Children's Books
MILWAUKEE

Animals are always on the alert. The Gray Squirrel keeps watch the entire time he is eating. High in a tree, he is safe from ground enemies, but he must keep watch for dangerous birds flying overhead.

Cautious House Mice take turns being on the lookout while feeding.

The water hole is a dangerous place. A lioness may be lurking in the bushes nearby, knowing that thirsty animals must come to drink because there is no other water for them for miles around. Animals never come to a water hole on their own if they can help it. They always come in herds. The more eyes, ears, and noses there are to detect danger, the safer the animals feel. While the zebras put their heads down, the Giraffes keep watch. If something startles the Giraffes, the zebras become frightened too, and run away to safety.

Pearl can protect herself by running away or by lashing out with her sharp claws and teeth. But her ten-day-old kitten, Benjamin, is too little to protect himself. Pearl looks after him and keeps him safe. She is purring now but will turn into a spitting, slashing fury if anyone hurts Benjamin.

Honey is sweet and gentle with her puppies. She licks Gem's face and cuddles Fan. Her pups are just eleven days old and quite helpless. They can crawl but cannot see and have no teeth. If they are threatened, Honey will leap to defend them, snarling and biting if necessary.

Many animals keep their babies safe in a warm nest while they are little and helpless. This Egyptian Gerbil gathers dry grass to make a nest in a burrow underground. If she senses danger, she will carry her babies one by one to a safer nest.

Baby Moorhens are born on top of a big mound of reeds. The first chicks stay in the nest until all the eggs have hatched. Then they splash into the water and swim after their parents, who watch over them and warn them when to hide.

Usually it is the mother fish who looks after the eggs, but sometimes the father is the baby sitter. The male Worm Pipefish is hard to find among the brown seaweed. He carries his eggs safely stuck to his belly.

In a fast-flowing stream, the male Bullhead guards his eggs under a large stone.

The female African Mouthbreeder carries her eggs in her mouth to keep them safe. When the babies hatch, she lets them out to swim and feed. If a big fish swims by, the babies rush back to her mouth. She gobbles them up, then carries them away to a safer place. Then she spits them all out again. She must be careful not to swallow any.

Some animals have homes where they can run for safety. Others carry their homes with them. The soft bodies of Garden Snails are covered with slime. Snails need to stay wet all the time, so they only come out of their shells at night or when it rains. During hot weather, they go back into their shells, safe from the drying sun.

The shell of the Painted Topshell is strong. If this snail sees a big fish coming, it quickly clamps down and shuts itself tightly into its shell.

The Red-eared Terrapin can tuck its head, legs, and tail right inside its shell to keep safe. Or it can plop into the water and swim away to hide.

All sorts of soft-bodied animals take over other animals' shells after the owners have finished with them.

The hermit crab's legs and claws are tough, but its body is very soft and is coiled to fit inside a snail shell. When danger is near, the crab retreats right inside its shell, closing the entrance with a claw. As the crab grows, it becomes too big for its shell, so it finds a larger one. It feels about inside the new shell with its claws to be sure it is empty, then quickly walks out of its tight old shell into the bigger new one.

A Common Octopus has caught a crab. It curls up safely inside a large triton shell to enjoy its meal.

Fish take refuge in any cracks and crannies they can find, so empty shells make good hiding places.

Blennies live in rock pools on the seashore. The smaller one has been hiding in the cast-off shell of a Shore Crab. The crab who left this empty shell did not die; it just changed its skin. A crab's skin is hard and rigid and does not grow with the crab like a snail's shell grows with the snail. The crab makes a soft, new skin inside the old one. The dead skin cracks and the crab backs out.

A Swan Mussel used to live inside this hinged shell, but it died. Something ate away its soft body. Now a pair of mouthbreeders take shelter in its shell.

An arrow-poison frog does not need to hide. Frog-eating animals leave it alone because its bright color warns them that it is poisonous. South American Indians put its poison on their arrowheads. The venom is so strong that if an arrow tipped with the poison just grazes the skin, the victim will die.

Horns over its eyes and on its snout make the Nose-horned Frog look fierce. No smaller animal is safe from this frog because anything that crawls near is snapped up into its wide mouth. The frog keeps itself from being eaten by looking so much like a dead leaf that it is invisible as long as it stays still!

Nasty insects are often brightly colored. Some that are black with red spots are very nasty.

The Red Blister Beetle sits on leaves in the bright sunshine. When picked up, it oozes poisonous fluid that burns the skin and makes painful blisters.

Most moths are brown and fly at night. Birds and bats like to eat them. The brightly colored Six-spot Burnet Moth buzzes about when the sun is shining. It sits on flowers and is easy for birds to see. But if a bird pecks one, yellow drops of acid ooze from the moth's neck. One taste and that bird will never touch another black-and-red insect again!

Wasps and hornets are almost all striped black and yellow. They are safe from attack because their stripes advertise that they sting. Everyone fears a wasp sting.

The Wasp Beetle has no sting, although it is striped like a wasp. It moves in a jerky wasplike way and looks very much like a Common Wasp. Birds leave it alone.

The harmless Ant Beetle also pretends to be a wasp. It looks like a different sort of wasp called a velvet ant, which is black and white and has a very bad sting.

Both of these beetles are quite harmless. They stay safe because they pretend to be harmful wasps.

A Bull's-eye Moth is hard to see when it rests on a tree with its wings closed. If something disturbs it, the moth flicks open its wings, suddenly flashing bright eyespots on its underwings. The eyespots look like the eyes of a large and menacing animal — perhaps a Saw-whet Owl, a dangerous bird of prey.

Hedgehogs are very prickly and have strong, sharp spines instead of soft fur on their backs. When startled, the first thing a hedgehog does is to put its head down and its prickles up. If a fox or a dog goes to sniff it, the hedgehog "huffs" and jerks. It pricks the predator on the nose! The wounded animal yelps and usually leaves the hedgehog alone. But if a really hungry fox still tries to bite it, the hedgehog quickly rolls up into a tight ball. Curled up like that, with prickles sticking out in all directions, a hedgehog is completely safe.

The old country name for the European Hedgehog was "urchin." Sea urchins are round and covered with sharp spines, like a curled-up hedgehog. The Hatpin Urchin has long spines. They are not only as sharp as needles but poisonous as well. If the Hatpin Urchin feels something with the tip of one spine, it points lots of other spines in the same direction.

The Diadem Urchin waves its spines as it walks over the rocks. It uses some of its short, stubby spines for walking, but its longer spines are weapons that keep the urchin safe.

White Rhinoceroses are huge beasts. They wallow in mud or dust. They don't bother anybody as long as nobody bothers them. If angry, however, they charge like tanks, and trample and gore other creatures. Because of their size and strength and bad temper, all the other animals leave rhinos alone.

But rhinos have enemies more dangerous than any lion — humans. Poachers kill rhinos whenever they can because their horns are worth a lot of money. Special wardens try to guard rhinos and keep them safe in game parks.

Fun Facts

1. Porcupines are covered with quills on their back and sides. This spiny armor provides a good defense against any attack.

2. Skunks are not the only animals that use odor as a weapon to ward off others. Insects like the stinkbug, bedbug, lacewing fly, and the cockroach also use this type of defense.

3. A fawn hides by lying down quietly on the ground. Its spotted coat blends with the leaves of the forest floor.

4. Some Arctic animals have white coats to match the color of the ice and snow of their home territory. This helps to protect and camouflage such animals as the Polar Bear, the baby Harp Seal, and the Arctic Fox.

5. The green tree frog and the poisonous tree snake stay safe by hiding among green leaves.

6. Some insects and other animals, such as the gecko, the katydid, and the Screech Owl, look like tree bark. They really seem to be part of the tree as long as they remain still.

7. One kind of caterpillar hides by putting bits of leaves on its back.

8. Octopuses find shelter in safe places. They live in the empty homes of other animals in undersea caves or between rocks.

9. The little lizard called a chameleon can change color to match its environment and to show anger or fear.

10. When a kangaroo defends itself, it sits back on its tail for balance and strikes at the enemy with its hind feet tipped with strong nails.

For More Information About Animal Life

These books and magazines will tell you many interesting things about animals. When possible, we have listed videos. Check your local library or bookstore to see if they have these materials or will order them for you.

Books:

Animal Camouflage. Penny (Franklin Watts)
Animal Homes. Elswit (Western)
Animals on the Move. Bevington (Wright Group)
Animals That Live in Shells. Morris (Raintree)
Animals That Migrate. Arnold (Carolrhoda Books)
Endangered Animals. Morris (Raintree)
Wildlife on the Watch. Adrian (Hastings)

Magazines:

Chickadee
Young Naturalist Foundation
P.O. Box 11314
Des Moines, IA 50340

Owl
Young Naturalist Foundation
P.O. Box 11314
Des Moines, IA 50340

National Geographic World
National Geographic Society
P.O. Box 2330
Washington, DC 20013-9865

Ranger Rick
National Wildlife Federation
8925 Leesburg Pike
Vienna, VA 22184-0001

Videocassettes:

Animal Babies. (Encyclopaedia Britannica Educational)
Animal Homes. (Churchill Films)

Things to Do

1. Many animals make their own shelters in order to keep safe. List animals you know that do this. Describe their special shelters.

2. Your home is a type of shelter. Make a list of things that you or your parents do to keep your home safe from danger.

3. Think of some of the ways cars and buses are designed to protect the driver and the passengers. List them.

4. What are some of the possible dangers of playing in a public park? What are some things you can do to be certain of your safety?

5. If you are playing with other children in your family, what are some of the ways you can help keep them safe from harm, whether you are playing indoors or outdoors?

6. Draw a picture of all the signs you can think of that help to keep you safe. Start with traffic signs and warning signs.

Things to Talk About

1. Most animals are always on the alert for danger. What exactly does this mean? Should people always be on the alert too? Why or why not?

2. Most animals know they must be cautious about possibly dangerous situations "instinctively." What does this mean? Are people usually cautious instinctively or is this something that must be learned?

3. Some animals have special places to hide in case of danger. Do you have a special place to go to in case of danger? Why is it a good idea to have one or two places in mind to be able to run to in a frightening situation?

4. What types of danger might there be when you go with some friends to a local shopping mall or to a festival? Discuss possible ways of keeping safe in these situations.

5. If you own a pet, explain how you help to keep it safe. Discuss the different types of dangers that might exist for different types of pets.

6. Sometimes keeping safe involves using all of your senses. Name the five senses and discuss ways in which using each one can help keep you safe from danger.

7. Sometimes children get into scary situations because they do not think carefully enough earlier about possible dangers. Have you ever been in a frightening situation because of this lack of careful thinking? Discuss your experience with your parents, teachers, and friends and try to figure out how thinking carefully could have helped you avoid what happened.

8. How do you decide whether it is wise or safe to trust people who are strangers to you? Discuss with your parents, classmates, and teachers ways to avoid dangerous strangers.

Glossary of New Words

bird of prey: a bird that catches, kills, and eats small mammals and other birds.

burrow: a hole or tunnel dug in the ground by an animal.

cautious: careful; wary.

cranny: a small, narrow opening or crack, as in a wall.

cuddle: to hold gently and lovingly; to embrace.

dangerous: unsafe; might cause pain or injury.

defend: to protect or guard from an enemy's attack.

detect: to discover something.

gobble: to eat quickly and greedily.

gore: to pierce, as with a tusk or horn.

hatch: to break out of or emerge from an egg.

lurk: to lie in wait; to move in a deliberately secretive way.

menacing: threatening, as if with harm or danger.

poacher: a person who hunts or fishes illegally while trespassing on someone else's property.

reeds: tall, slender grasses that grow in wet or marshy land.

refuge: a place of safety, shelter, or retreat.

retreat: to withdraw from a threatening situation to a place of safety.

startle: to surprise or frighten suddenly or unexpectedly.

threaten: to give signs of inflicting pain or harm.

wallow: to roll about in mud, dirt, or water.

Index

acid 20
Ant Beetle 21
arrow-poison frog 18
arrowheads 18

baby sitter 12
bats 20
birds 20, 21
Blennies 17
Bull's-eye Moth 22
bullhead 12
burrow 10

cats 9
chicks 10
claws 9, 16
Common Octopus 16
Common Wasp 21

dogs 9, 24

eggs 12, 13
Egyptian Gerbil 10
eyespots 22

fish 17
fox 24
fur 24

game parks 26
Giraffes 7

grass 10
Gray Squirrel 4

head 15
hedgehogs 24, 25
hermit crabs 16
hornets 21
horns 19, 26
House Mice 5

insects 20

legs 15, 16
lions 7

Moorhens 10
moths 20
mouth 19
mouthbreeders 17
    African 13

Nose-horned frog 19
noses 7, 24

poachers 26
poison 8, 20, 25
predator 24

Red Blister Beetle 20
Red-eared Terrapin 15
reeds 10

Saw-whet Owl 22
shells 15, 26, 17
Shore Crab 17
Six-spot Burnet Moth 20
skin 17, 18
snail
    Garden 15
    Painted Topshell 15
    shell 16
snout 19
South American Indians 18
spines 24, 25
sun 15, 20
Swan Mussel 17

urchins
    Diadem 25
    Hatpin 25
    Sea 25

velvet ant 21

Wasp Beetle 21
wasps 21
water 10, 15
water holes 7
White Rhinoceroses 26
wings 22
Worm Pipefish 12

zebras 7